Woolgathering

T0001800

The Woolgatherers

There was a field. There was a hedge
composed of great bushes framing my view.
The hedge I regarded as sacred - the
stronghold of the spirit. The field I
revered as well, with its high beckoning
grass and powerful bend. The field of God.

Beyond, to the right, was a small peach
orchard and to the left a white washed
barn with the words HOE-DOWN HALL
above the double door. On Sunday evenings
we all would meet and dance to the
fiddler and the fiddler's call.

Later, after my bath, my mother would
comb my hair and I'd say my
prayers and she'd tuck me in. I'd
wait til all was quiet. Then I'd
rise, mount a chair, push aside the
cloth that covered my window and
continue my prayers; wandering, to
greet my god.

On clear, peculiar nights I sometimes
saw movement in the grasses. At first
I thought it to be the swipe of the white
owl or great pale wings of the luna
moth that seemed to spread and fold
like a medieval habit. But it came to
me one night that it was people, like
none I had ever saw, in strange archaic
dress. I used to think I could see
the white of their bonnets and, at times,
a hand, in the act of grasping.

Woolgathering

·

Patti Smith

A NEW DIRECTIONS BOOK

PUBLISHER'S NOTE: Portions of this book were originally published in a 1992 Hanuman Books edition of *Woolgathering*.

Illustration credits begin on page 93.

First published in cloth in 2011 and as New Directions Paperbook 1512 in 2021 with a new afterword by the author (ISBN 978-0-8112-3125-1)
Manufactured in the United States of America
Design by Erik Rieselbach

Library of Congress Cataloging-in-Publication Data
Smith, Patti.
Woolgathering / Patti Smith.
p. cm.
ISBN 978-0-8112-1944-0 (hardcover : alk. paper)
1. Smith, Patti—Childhood and youth. I. Title.
PS3569.M53787Z46 2011
811'.54—dc22
[B]   2011023578

10 9 8 7 6 5 4 3 2

New Directions Books are published for James Laughlin
by New Directions Publishing Corporation
80 Eighth Avenue, New York 10011

For my father

Contents

To the reader

In 1991 I lived on the outskirts of Detroit with my husband and two children in an old stone house set by a canal that emptied into Lake Saint Clair. Ivy and morning glory climbed the deteriorating walls. A profusion of grapevines and wild roses draped the balcony, where doves nested in their tangles. The yard was a bit overgrown, much to our neighbors' consternation, and they would often try to tame it while we were away. Our unruly patch boasted an abundance of wildflowers, lilacs, two ancient willows, and a single pear tree. I truly loved my family and our home, yet that spring I experienced a terrible and inexpressible melancholy. I would sit for hours, when my chores were done and the children at school, beneath the willows, lost in thought. That was the atmosphere of my life as I began to compose *Woolgathering*.

I had received a letter from Raymond Foye, who cofounded Hanuman Books with Francesco Clemente, requesting a

manuscript. A Hanuman Book was only 3 by 4 inches in size, like a tiny Indian prayer book that one could carry in one's pocket. Charmed by the prospect, I began my task in early fall, just as the pears were forming. I wrote slowly at first and Raymond would call every so often to encourage me. One afternoon he called to relay a request from William Burroughs. All Hanuman Books were numbered on the spine and mine was to be 46, the year of my birth. But William desired it, as his favorite number was 23, which doubled to mine. For the love of William I traded with him.

I wrote by hand on sheets of graph paper, and on December 30, 1991, on my forty-fifth birthday, I completed the manuscript. I sent it off to Raymond, who typed it out for me and sent it to Madras to be published. As it turned out 45 was the perfect number for me.

I gave my father the first copy of *Woolgathering*, but as time passed he said nothing. My father was a beautiful man but difficult to impress and I only halfheartedly hoped he would read it. Yet some years later, shortly before his death, he said to me, "Patricia, I have read your book." I prepared myself for certain criticism, but was struck that he called such a small offering a book. "You're a good writer," he said, and he made me a cup of coffee. It was the only such compliment he ever gave me.

Someone asked if I would consider *Woolgathering* a fairy tale. I have always adored such tales but I am afraid it does not qualify. Everything contained in this little book is true, and written just like it was. The writing of it drew me from my strange torpor and I hope that in some measure it will fill the reader with a vague and curious joy.

PALM SUNDAY, 2011, BARCELONA

WOOLGATHERING

A Bidding

I always imagined I would write a book, if only a small one, that would carry one away, into a realm that could not be measured nor even remembered.

I imagined a lot of things. That I would shine. That I'd be good. I'd dwell bareheaded on a summit turning a wheel that would turn the earth and undetected, amongst the clouds, I would have some influence; be of some avail.

Curious wishes feathered the air making light the limbs of a somber, spindle-legged child barely able to keep her anklets from disappearing into her heavy shoes.

All my socks were out of shape. Possibly because I often filled them with marbles. I'd load them with aggies and steelies and head out. It was the one thing I was good at and I could beat anyone around.

At night I'd pour my booty upon my bed and wipe them with a chamois. I'd arrange them by color, by order of merit, and they'd rearrange themselves — small glowing planets, each with its own history, its own will of gold.

I never had a sense that the ability to win came from me. I always felt it was in the object itself. Some piece of magic that was animated through my touch. In this manner I found magic in everything, as if all things, all of nature bore the imprint of a jinn.

You had to be careful, you had to be wise. For the discerning might catch something far away and draw it close.

And the wind caught the edges of the cloth that covered my window. There I kept vigil, alert to the small, easily becoming, through an open eye, monstrous and beautiful.

I would gaze, gauge and just like that, be gone — vane avion, flitting from earth to earth, unconscious of my awkward arms or wayward socks.

I was off and not a soul was aware. For it appeared to all that I was still among them, upon my little bed, rapt in child's play.

The Woolgatherers

There was a field. There was a hedge composed of great bushes framing my view. The hedge I regarded as sacred — the stronghold of the spirit. The field I revered as well, with its high, beckoning grass and powerful bend.

Beyond, to the right, was an orchard, and to the left a white-washed barn with the words HOEDOWN HALL above the double doors. Here, on Sunday evenings, we all would meet and dance to the fiddler and the fiddler's call.

Later, after my bath, my mother would comb my hair and I'd say my prayers and she'd tuck me in. I'd wait till all was quiet. Then I'd rise, mount a chair, push aside the cloth that covered my window and continue my prayers, wandering, to greet my God.

On clear, peculiar nights I sometimes saw movement in the grasses. At first I thought it to be the swipe of the white owl

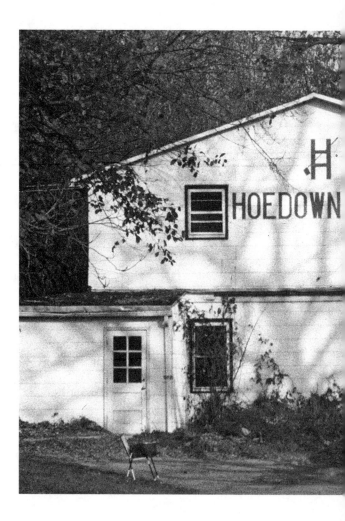

or the great pale wings of a luna moth spreading and folding like a medieval habit. But it came to me one night that they were people like none I had ever seen, in strange archaic cap and dress. I used to think I could see the white of their bonnets and, at times, a hand, in the act of grasping, illuminated by the moon and stars or the light from a passing car.

Morning found the field bright, abundant with a thousand wildflowers we often gathered and wove into crowns. But the center-piece was the old black barn inhabited by bats. It has long since burned, But at that time it stood like a battered top hat that only the courageous or forlorn might wear.

We'd pass it on our walks, my brother, sister and I. I was the eldest, the youngest not yet born. We'd walk to the center of town and scale the stone wall that protected, like a mother's arms, the Cemetery of Friends. Beneath the great walnut trees the brethren came to rest, and it seemed to us, even by day, to be the most discreet and silent place on earth. Here, enveloped by an air both solemn and sweet, we puffed on the punks we cut from the swamp, communing for hours yet not saying a word. These times filled us with joy. Volumes of joy that still pleasure me in the reading.

Skipping home we'd salute all that charmed us. The old man who sold minnows. The creek that seemed so wide it might have opened into the mouth of the Delaware. The armory, the hall, and then Thomas' Field greeting us, seeming to call us by name.

We raced through the grass, meeting up with our friends. Sometimes I'd just plop deep within it and stare up at the sky.

It seemed like all of creation was mapped out above and I was drawn from the laughter of the other children into a stillness I aspired to master. Here one could hear a seed form or the soul fold like a handkerchief.

I believed they were there, the people. I could hear them, now and then, murmuring and whistling as if behind a wall of cotton. I could hear them but I could never make out the language they were speaking nor the melodies they were weaving.

When I'd return everything was as it was, I'd run and join the others and we'd play statue and red rover or if we were feeling brave venture into the barn and pitch sticks at the bats. Later, crossing the road home, I never failed to bow my head as we passed the bush.

One afternoon I was sent to town alone. I was in an agitated state for I had decided to ask the old man who sold

minnows about the people in the field, Children feared him but in a certain light he seemed almost blessed, eternal. The oldest man in the oldest house — a tumbling shack, painted black and set back in an overgrown patch. The word BAIT was stenciled on the tilting roof. Here he sat, in all weather, in his overalls, long white hair and beard, keeping watch over the world and the grave of his wife buried in the shadows by the house.

I stood there by him. It seemed to me I never really asked. For my mind, darting this way and that, would not cooperate with my tongue. But perhaps a phrase or two escaped. For he answered, as he turned the bowl of his pipe without opening his eyes, without so much as moving his lips:

They be the woolgatherers ...

I didn't question beyond that. It seemed too fragile, too important. I just lit out, fairly flew, scarcely remembering to say goodbye. I did turn to wave as I ran and his open eyes caught mine and seemed to contain that which one might only call a splendor.

I was not at all sure what a woolgatherer was but it sounded a worthy calling and seemed a good job for me. And so I kept watch. In every weather. Then I drew the cloth and lay upon my bed, unable to sleep, amusing myself by giving them names and designing, by the beam of my pocket flash, their cloaks and boots and the clouds they called home.

And the image of the woolgatherers in that sleepy field drew me to sleep as well. And I wandered among them, through thistle and thorn, with no task more exceptional than to rescue a fleeting thought, as a tuft of wool, from the comb of the wind.

Barndance

The mind of a child is like a kiss on the forehead — open and disinterested. It turns as the ballerina turns, atop a party cake with frosted tiers, poisonous and sweet.

The child, mystified by the commonplace, moves effortlessly into the strange, until the nakedness frightens, confounds, and he seeks a bit of cover, order. He glimpses, he gleans; piecing together a crazy quilt of truths — wild and woolly ones, hardly bordering on truth at all.

The cruel intensity of this process can produce a thing of beauty but oftentimes just a tear in the shimmering from which to wrest and wriggle. A spine of rope sliding an arena more remote and dazzling than ever.

All around are walls, and the mind, in vague pirouette, snatches bits of code — Flemish, hieroglyph chiseled in the brick.

Exclamations! Questions of origin, scope.

When young, overcome with a sense of being from somewhere else, we peer, we probe inside and pull out alien, indian. We come upon an open plain, A plain of gold. Or
come, most often, upon a cloud, A race of cloud dwellers.
These are our young thoughts.

Eventually we work it out. We recognize, in ourselves, our
mother's hand, our father's limb. But the mind, that is something else again. Of this one can never be sure.

For it turns as the wild dog turns, as the tumbleweed, the
wire rim. This aspect of our being is transmutable and perhaps where we find the true kink in the machine. Mind is a
picture. And there in the corner is the hint of a spiral. Perhaps it is a virus; perhaps it is a spirit tattoo.

With arms outstretched
with eyes closed tight
a bright nausea
turns all around
stirring hearts
wistful sprouts
turning themselves
inside out

How wide the world is. How high. And the stuff of the mind — charged, poofs and scatters like seed and fluff. For such is the tooth of the lion. That it bares and bursts into wishes.

A wish for a certain thing
or just the wish to know.

Blowing upon it, candles, a star ... What does one desire. A partner. A freewheeling moon. Or perhaps to hear again as one heard as a child. A music — curious, optimistic, as plain and elusive as the call of the reel permeating a summer night. Expanding squares of laughter and delight. Everyone dancing, just dancing.

And out there one would be drawn, like the moth and the firefly, into a distorted calm. The hall, strung with colored lights, fading ... as one would venture into the high grass, lured by another call — such a pretty wailing, like a violin in bloom.

The music of the woolgatherers performing their task. Bending, extending, shaking out the air. Gathering what needs to be gathered. The discarded. The adored. Bits of human spirit that somehow got away. Caught up in an apron. Plucked by a gloved hand.

From all this the cloud is formed. And so the sky resembles the human opera. The turbulent promenade. It attracts the lazy eye. It appeases the weary in a play of movements heralding the simple.

The woolgatherers performing their task. Without wage or contract; with singular, collective grace.

It is one of those inexplicable things. For it is a service one enters without expectation or design. Where one, lost in thought, may feel a tap upon the shoulder and find oneself far flung, in a swirl of dust, swung about and brought to a sudden halt.

With such a burden lifted, such a glory in the hand and racing anticipation as if one had an appointment, a do-si-do, with the setting sun.

Cowboy Truths   *for Sam Shepard*

Relaxed, beneath the sky, contemplating this and that. The
nature of labor. The nature of idleness and the sky itself with
billowing masses so close one might lasso a cloud to pil-
low one's head or fill one's belly. Sopping up the beans and
gravy with a chunk of cloud meat and lying back for a little
siesta. What a life!

A day of power. It's his birthday. And in this rare, deli-
cious atmosphere he breathes. He was born as the campfire
burned and the red hawk, circled, His mother carried him
on her back and his father rocked him to sleep to the strains
of a rugged ballad.

Careful how you bare yer soul
Careful not to bare it all

He awakes with a start, aimless wrangler, brimming with
goodwill and itching to mosey on. He hoists his burden
over his shoulder. His own manner of life, his own end.

Atrocious and radiant that it may be. He has accepted the majesty of his lot with an unquestioning heart and his gift lies unwrapped before him: freedom, mean freedom.

He has given all away save for one part. This blessed speck, this lone lariat, he has saved for himself. Save some for yerself, he drawls amidst a fit of laughter. For if you're aiming at spitting at the sky better do it with a grin.

Standing there, squinting in the sun; everything so damn beautiful, enough to make the throat ache. He scans the terrain, the palm of his hand and that golden nuisance for one small moment of truth. And this is what he's found.

Himself, in a labor of love, clearing land, pulling debris from a river, mending its bed. Seldom tiring — filled with a crazy kind of hope. He answers to no one and no one proclaims.

You are not forgotten.
That's his word.
His one great truth.
As he reenacts
the rituals of youth.
Putting things right.
A dusty piece of humanity.
Heaven's hired hand.

Indian Rubies   *for Paul Getty*

I have always possessed a kind of knapsack, if nothing more than a piece of cloth or skin tied in a knot. My sack, worthy companion, produces, when opened, a world defined by its contents — fluxion, unique, beloved.

This uncommon bundle has always been my comfort, my happy burden. Yet I have found it unwise to attach myself to the souvenirs within. For as soon as I focus on a certain object I misplace it or it just disappears.

I had a ruby. Imperfect, beautiful like faceted blood. It came from India where they wash up on the shore. Thousands of them — the beads of sorrow. Little droplets that some-how became gems gathered by beggars who trade them for rice. Whenever I stared into its depths I felt overcome, for caught within my little gem was more misery and hope than one could fathom.

It frightened and inspired, and I kept it in my sack, a waxed yellow packet the size and shape of a razor blade. I'd stop and take it out and look at it. I did this so often it was no longer necessary to see what I was looking at. And because of this I can not say for certain when it disappeared.

I can still see it though. I see it on the foreheads of the women. In the poet's hollow. I see it at the throat of a diva and in the palm of the deserter. Pressing against a wire fence. A drop of blood on a calico dress. I open my bundle and dump the contents in the furrows of the earth. Nothing — an old spoon, a rudder, the remains of a walkie-talkie. Spreading the cloth to rest upon I take breaths as long as the furrows. As if to quell the spirits; hold them from shaking and clanging.

In the ring of the impossible night. Everything elastic. The sky a deep disturbing rose. I can feel the dust of Calcutta, the gone eyes of Bhopal. I can see the prayer flags flapping about like old socks in the warm, ironic wind.

Can I offer you this bell
the whisper merchant
It is extremely valuable
a museum piece, priceless
No thank you, I answer
I do not wish to own
But it is a wonderful bell
a ceremonial piece
a fine bell
My head is a bell
I murmur
between
bandaged fingers
already asleep

IN CONGRESS, JULY

...mous Declaration ... States

When in the Course of human events...

Drawing

The Ghosts of Ayler popped and pitted. It gave me a kick-sound, like fingers, poking game little holes in a spread of tight net. Dictionaries littered the floor — Spanish, Arabic … Omas inks, sheets of vellum, E.S.P. discs, sacred sticks, spangled cloth and *Poems of a Millionaire*. Poet debris. Crazy booty I often inventoried in the dead of night,

The document curled in the heavy air. A parchment repro of the Declaration acquired on a third grade expedition to the Franklin Institute, 1955. It ranked high in my treasure. The audacious grace of the script intrigued me and I spent hours as a child copying it out — the image of the word, the signatures — on long paper scrolls. I imagined that in mastering each bold, significant hand, I would capture some of the spirit of the author, of Independence itself.

Now here, spurred by Ayler, I repeated my grave little game. I had no aptitude for languages so I learned instead to copy out the image of a language. Pages of calligraphy scattered about like wires of the world. I got up just as a new side dropped. Patty Waters — "Black is the Color." Some said she was dead. Some said she sold tickets in a B-movie theater. In any event she could sing. A voice like smoke.

The pot was boiling over. I got up and strained a fist full of mint and poured the liquid in a favorite cup. It resembled an inverted fez, having no handles, a glowing milky glaze swimming with fish and phoenix. It had held, in its time, the drink of transport for a dervish, then an Englishman, and now myself. I filled it again and returned to my station, I sat there for a long time with my tea, dressed in my green raincoat that clashed with everything in the room. It was an absurd thing that I adored, of rubberized kelly taffeta, picked up in a rich heap somewhere. I sat in the changing light in the center of the room, copying out the Lord's Prayer in Aramaic, hoping something would be revealed in the process.

Another side dropped. The last on the stack. Fra Angelico. There were several picture books on the shelf and I chose one at random — a small series of charcoal drawings by Willem de Kooning, done with closed eyes. Vigorous, astute. A few in crucifixion posture, all figurative springing into the abstract.

Inspired, I pulled out my pencils and a pad of claycoat. I made several small drawings in a manner I learned from Robert — a field composed of a single word — a simple phrase repeated, entwining. And then, as was my wont, more elaborate phrases snaking back to a single line, I worked freely, for a long time, imagining him appraising, over my shoulder, saying simply — It works. It doesn't work.

I was pleased with my small suite of drawings. I taped a few on the wall next to a newspaper picture of Fernando Pessoa and a snapshot of my mother standing before a great pile of felled trees, smiling. "Me by the Timbers, Chattanooga 1942" in her own hand. I cleaned up and stored my stuff, for suddenly I craved order. I poured another tea and turned the record over. Ho Ho Hovhaness. All Men are Brothers. I sat on my second-story fire escape and watched the people pass into dusk.

I laid my raincoat across the foot of my mat and chose an old muslin dress to sleep in. It was a warm evening. I said my prayers and pushed the arm of the player over. Then the record would play over and over as I slept.

All Men are Brothers. Would that it were true. And the sailor could sleep peacefully in the crater of the desert and the Moslem in the arms of a Christian ship. I slept for so long a time that the vendors serving afternoon lunch had already departed when I awoke.

It was a humid, vaporous afternoon and though in good humor, my wrists, my entire being, was aware of the approaching storm. In the corner was a cylindrical tub I used, inverted, as a table for my dorje, a traveling box, a silver offering bowl, and a small but very old butterlamp. I removed them carefully and wrapped them in cloth. Then I wiped out the tub, filled it with very hot water and brown salt and bathed a long while. The salt drew the pain from my limbs and after a simple meal of bread and coffee I brought out my sewing basket. It was my intention to make a quilt for my brother — a cowboy patchwork. But as I worked by hand, slowly and with little skill, he would most likely suffer several winters without it.

I enjoyed the task not only out of love for my brother but for each patch, for all were remnants of our childhood or some spirited place. The plaid of our shirts, my sister's dotted swiss, brown flannel from Nepal, satin moiré from Robert's studio, gingham, velvets … each square transporting as a wild seed or a rare cup of tea. I confess, however, the undertaking made me drowsy and I drifted to a place that seemed more present than myself, sitting, dutifully sewing as my fingers let slip the thread and joined my mind, elsewhere.

iii

I entered a familiar terrain not unlike the city of Rey. Dwellings — geometric shapes — carved in the steppes of an arid landscape, all with windows no greater than a hand. I went from place to place issuing lengths of heavy gauze, to be rationed out as mosquito nets. But some of the women used the netting for veils and others dropped them into vats of dye made from the henna plant. They spread them out, a bright green that dried a faded violet in the sun. To these they attached spangles cut from thin sheets of mica. They wore them like shawls and danced on the rooftops. Some of the spangles dropped like fallen stars and I caught them and slipped them into my coat pocket.

The children followed me, gripping the hem of my coat, begging for coins and candy. It seemed endless, my task — endless lengths of netting, endless windows in the shape of great hands pressed into rows and rows of spartan housing.

At last I reached the end and I followed a path that led to the river. The women had already collected their water and I was left alone. I leaned against a cypress tree to rest, Far away, upon the water, were boats, scores of little wooden boats with immaculate sails. The fleet an enormous child, leaning over a cloud and setting them down, one by one, delicate as a wing. I saw not a soul, felt not a breath of humanity, yet the sails multiplied, overwhelming the horizon — one unblemished expanse. I closed my eyes, seized with the desire to dip a quivering twig into a pool of ink and draw upon it as one would draw a bow across a string.

When I opened my eyes I was surrounded by children taunting and laughing, I stood up and they pounced on the coins that had fallen from my pocket. I went on my way but something brushed my heart and I turned as one of the children, a small girl, smiled and waved. The sky was growing dark and the boats were no more than bits of wood — popsicle sticks floating in a puddle after a rain.

I had one of those headaches. It kept pounding and got into that crazy realm where the guillotine seems like a good idea. I groped about for the scissors and just like that cropped my hair. Brushing aside the discarded braids I dragged over to the sink to cool my face and neck. Then curled back on the mat feeling somewhat free, and slid gratefully into sleep.

I awoke in the center of night. Above my head, beyond the open skylight was the moon — a vibrant gold — like the shield of a frightened but determined young warrior.

How still everything seemed
how elaborately still
and all I could think of lying there
as I bounded from hill to hill
was the phrase
"In movement is blessing"

A cloud pulled across the moon. Black radiance. Newborn blind I felt about for my journal and laid there holding it, waiting for the moon to reappear and shed some light.

The ceiling was a grid, hairy
with swooping line, muscle
another tongue
but not that of language

Wading a shallow pool.... Turning I saw a white horse on a green field and a red horse on a white field. Unable to choose I laid back and floated, like a bloom in a bowl. The pages of my journal spread a mocking shadow across the calm surface. I stood up. The sky was a bright, unbroken blue. I knew the horse I wanted. I knew as if struck by the point of a ragged spear.

I was not an expert rider but I was no stranger either. Some hopsack was caught in the bush. I covered my horse's back and mounted.

"In movement is blessing"

This phrase, like a musical air, turned in my ear as we rode. I could feel the wind on my neck, naked where I had cropped my hair.

All about was net, above and beneath, closing in as we rode until we could ride no longer. I dismounted and continued on foot. No walls, no planes. Just a network of billowing corridors. They opened onto the enclosed; each equipped with some piece of distraction.

On the screen the performer in the act of dancing embraces the monkey god, the mischievous deity, the slender shade, boy to beast to shackled rose — something of us all.

The drowned to the risen — drawn through the tightening net like venom from a wound.

The net dropped, laden with fish, pearls, the cremated leaf ...

I had a fleeting impression of my horse being led to an abrupt, official end. I vowed to honor him in a work — something insignificant, eternal.

A white drawing depicting the jilted air. After the departing of birds. The white anguish photographed by Rimbaud as he crossed the St. Gotthard Pass. The gauze the dead weep into.

A white drawing to adorn the blank wall of an outpost, or the deserted café.

The pot boiled over. I strained a fist full of mint and poured. To wash away all ills so they become as a footnote. We walk over the burning slag. It seems there is nothing we cannot do. We are hailed in the market place. We beat on the bongo; we blow on the reed. To portray the delicate; to shatter nature.

I examined my walls papered in childish script. Once, I found myself stirred, by a contour, an apron string. Certain things and the form of things. A white starched collar. Great hands against a dark coat. To rid myself of these disturbing proportions I drew, and after a time the drawing itself took on a prominence relative to nothing. It became a work, a torture I soon abandoned.

I placed the last of my tools — quills — in a box. I pressed my palms together and bowed, leaving my post in pursuit of life noise. My window opened onto a fire escape overlooking

the street. People were scurrying, winged. It was Christmas
I imagined. Soon we would bend to the whims of the sun.
Soon the leaves, like dying hands, would fall. The wind in
its wisdom had filled my own. A one-way pass from Darjeel-
ing to Ghum. I pressed my palms together holding tight my
prize, alive like the egg of a mayfly. Drawing close to the rail,
I let drop my cloak, and the contents showered. My hair fell
in greasy braids down my back.

The only thing you can count on is change.

Two Worlds

I fired up a pan of Joan of Arc beans; poured olive oil over some shredded lettuce and opened a bottle of Gatorade. I was hungry so I stood as I ate, then scraped my plate and left it in the sink. Sated I shifted gears, rummaging around until I found what I was looking for — a film cassette of Cocteau's *Orphée* — which I shoved in the player, fast-forwarding to the part about the death of Cégeste — Orphée's intoxicated and scornful young rival. Pausing on an image of the Café des Poètes, I shrugged off the present and freely entered as the action heated up against a soundtrack of motorcycles and bongos. I leaned against the wall facing the exit, zeroing in on Juliette Gréco's bangs and Beat sweater, as Orphée sang bitterly from another universe.

I was satisfied to note that I was dressed exactly like the drunken poet — shirt opened at the neck (though his was soon to be spattered with blood), rolled trousers, leather shoes, no socks. Moving past the bar I paused to look at my reflection. My collar was stained from the deep red juice of the kidney beans, a perfect match.

I downed a coffee then stepped into the light, attempting to extract myself, cell by cell, from the increasingly unstable scene. I had no desire to witness yet again the indifferent snuffing of modern poetry. I figured to stop at the Two Worlds, but as I approached the unremarkable façade I hesitated, there were too many people — students mostly. They poured out into the street waving the flags of the future. I felt I knew them, but I also felt they would not know me — a mere intruder spirited through a dusty glass from a realm where a transistor dictates the sublime.

I slipped my hand in my pocket and found a wad of notes — pounds, marks and Swiss francs. I could feel the restless, belligerent aspects of my personality surfacing. I stepped into a tobacconist and picked up a Bic, a journal, and a Hav-A-Hank. It seemed I had a small wound in my neck and my shirt was becoming quite wet. I tried to wipe the stain from my collar, but it spread instead. A kid was hawking papers: SNOW IN THE DESERT. I entered the café unnoticed; the unaccountable wound was my ticket in.

I opened the journal intending to write but drew instead. The atmosphere was tolerable and I soon became engrossed in my work, blotting out the whispers and laughter that tended to make me uneasy. I sketched out a shield, divided into three horizontal panels, marking the top with the letter *A* and an *O* at the bottom. The center panel was a pre-existing landscape where phrases laced the high grass. I had it in my mind that if I peered long enough I'd make them out, coming up with the words that would set this place on its ear. Kneeling, I collected what I could as the blades sliced through my threadbare trousers, issuing small streams that trickled from the edge of the table onto the speckled linoleum. Surrounded by onlookers I divvied out pastel-colored notes from an overflowing egg basket — the spoils of a disturbed bunny.

Suddenly I was tired. The jukebox was a mix of elevator jazz and sixties garage rock. *Riot on Sunset Strip* was projected on the back wall and a dosed Mimsey Farmer, writhing in a flowered mini dress, was about to be nailed by several hopped-up hipsters. The Seeds permeated the air. I picked up my stuff and left, leaving several pounds on the table. The waiter rushed after me.

"What's this?" he said, waving the notes.

"Oh, sorry," I said, extending my wad.

He peeled off a few bills and shook his head.

It occurred to me that I wasn't sure where the hell I was.

Everything was familiar, foreign. I stopped at the Café Isabelle looking for a phone book. There were several stacked in a corner. Pictures of the young adventurer in her sailor garb and Arab dress were tacked on the wall behind an impressive coffee urn. A kid was hawking papers: FLASH FLOOD IN THE DESERT. Oblivious to onlookers I removed her image but it turned to dust in my hand. I ordered a Turkish coffee but did not drink it, as I suddenly wanted something stronger.

Nothing, yet everything, clicked. I circled back to the Two Worlds, though the interior had changed. Even the cigarette smoke seemed different. It was a lot like the Café des Poètes — table revolutionaries and pallbearers. I ordered a Pernod and water. I no longer cared about anything. Sitting at the bar was a Modigliani with chestnut hair piled high in a topknot that enhanced her long pale neck. She mouthed the words *So long* and I realized that I hadn't talked to anyone save waiters and shopkeepers for several days. I looked at my watch. It hadn't been wound, a pity, for I had neither the time nor sense of time.

A late lunch of fruit and milk.

I had scribbled that on the inside of my wrist but the thought was repellent. I ordered another Pernod and water, but what I really wanted was to lie down. I lost a lot of blood and some had dripped on the page of my journal. *The tears of Pollock*, I explained to the waiter. *The tears of Pollock* I scrawled across the page. The drips multiplied forming a fence of slim jagged poles. The lines I had written multiplied as well. I could not tame them and my entire station was noticeably vibrating, as if teeming with newborn caterpillars. Quickly I drained my glass and motioned for another. I tried to focus on a portrait behind the brass cash register. Flemish fifteenth-century. I had seen it somewhere before, perhaps in the hall of a local guild. The sight of it produced a shudder and then a curious rush of warmth. It was her head covering. A fragile habit framing her face like the folding wings of a large diaphanous moth.

I laid my possessions on the table — foreign coins, my wad, a rabbit's foot, a Bic, and a gem concealed in a yellow packet. I opened it with some difficulty. There it was, a minute, primary vowel. I RED. I rose to leave. The poets were sizing me up. A shield the thickness of a journal lay at my feet. With some degree of self-mockery, I offered it up. It struck me as I made my way to the door that I had enacted this before. Mirrored action with a shift of contents — a palette shape a seal brush bits of chalk.

I considered becoming a painter but I didn't have the stuff. I stumbled out as several students pulled on the coat tails of the ragged coat I had found at a makeshift stall in Camden Town that sold used boots and greatcoats and relics of war. They disbanded after rifling my paltry loot, murmuring like indiscernible bees. Worn phrases stung at me, simultaneous with a looping Doublemint jingle. I leaned against the brick for several minutes overcome with the sudden appearance of the sun and an overwhelming desire for a stick of gum.

I noticed the Café Dante was straight ahead. A kid hawking papers: ONE DOESN'T BECOME ONE IS. I knew where I was. Just beyond were the green double doors of the Gun Club. I plucked the strings of my gone shoes smack into love. If I walked straight, I'd hit the wide boulevard, so I turned the corner that led into a narrow passageway. It was opportune for abruptly everything came up, beans bobbing in a green fluorescent liquid, as if a plunger had released all the poisons of a plugged-up sink.

I steadied myself. Unearthing a stale stick of Black Jack from the depths of a pocket, I felt whole again. Taking deep breaths I crossed the street of cafes to the street of monochrome dreams and paused before an open window. A woman bent over linen. Strands of hair escaping from her pins, a wave loosening parallel to her arm as she pressed a heavy iron. I had the sudden urge to unburden all, to be nothing. I wanted to cry out but I couldn't. My breath formed language, but no sound, while the clear sky crisscrossed with fading remnants of prayers and poems trailing as though from the prop plane of Apollinaire.

I dreamed of being a painter, but I let the image slide into a vat of pigment and pastry-foam while I bounded from temple to junkyard in pursuit of the word. A solitary shepherdess gathering bits of wool plucked by the hand of the wind from the belly of a lamb. A noun. A nun. A red. O blue. Twittering threads caught in the thorns of an icy branch. Running in place, a ghost in vague expanse, I opened my arms to the sovereign trees and submitted to their pure, unholy embrace.

Art in Heaven

Navigating the feathered terrain dropping phrases like
"I've been in worse places
I've been in better
I've been around ..."
And all you want is a helping hand.
To be lifted out of the mire, out of beauty.
To be lifted ...

I let fly the windows, overlooking the river where the children draw water and the women pound their husbands'
shirts with a stone. Children, half naked, biting into strange
fruit, deliriously sweet, sing:

One day we shall all be dead
But those who keep moving
Tracing and retracing their steps
They shall never die
They shall be called
Rembrandt, Magellan

I dreamed of being a missionary.
I dreamed of being a mercenary.
My knapsack was a width of linen
tied like a pump on a stick.

Looking up, clouds form and reform. They resemble —
an embryo, a departed friend resting horizontal. Or a great
arm, compassionate as a spring, that if so ordained might
reach and take up that linen sack and all gathered within, if
only but the soul of an idea — the color of water, the weight
of a hill.

Nineteen Fifty-Seven

His name was Harry Riehl, a good name for a detective, but he seemed more shaman than detective. He would sit, in all weathers, in the dry patch in front of his slightly tilted house, with black shingles that made it look two-dimensional. He sat next to painted orange crates and sold bait, mostly minnows and worms. I never saw him anywhere else and only saw him get up once and enter his black shape of a shack and seemingly disappear.

His wife had died in 1947 and he buried her in their yard. This seemed to me an ultimate expression of being free; to be able to choose where to bury someone you love. I imagined he was sitting there, not only to sell bait, but as her guardian. He watched over her and because she was near to him, he was also near to her.

I always looked forward to catching a glimpse of him, holy as he was. I wasn't supposed to go into town alone but my mother would occasionally take me to Woodbury to get the Broad Street bus to Camden. We would pass him and he would give me a nod. Sometimes it might be no more than a wrinkle of an eye, but I knew it was for me.

In the summer of 1957 my youngest sibling Kimberly was born. She came ten years after me and was a surprise to everyone, including my mother. I remember my parents leaving for the hospital. There was a commercial for paper towels on TV from the Kimberly-Clark Company, and that is what my mother named her. My mother said when she saw her face, she knew she had seen that face before, but couldn't place it. Then she realized it was her own face. Kimberly was a sunny child, though she had severe asthma and a host of allergies.

In our little house, we were now eight, including my mother's cat Mittens and my dog Bambi. My mother loved her cat, and I loved Bambi as myself. My dog was a good companion, intelligent, quiet, and obedient. We had brought her with us when we left Germantown to start a new life in southern New Jersey.

My father used to go to the barbershop, when he had some extra change, to get a haircut. His barber sometimes let me sit in the big chair and he'd trim my bangs. Somehow they were never even. One day he brought a basket of puppies into the barbershop. His miniature Collie had mated with a German Shepherd. All the pups were longhaired, except for the runt of the litter. She had the coat of a Shepherd but the markings of a Collie. She resembled a small deer, so sweet and vulnerable in the basket, and I called her Bambi.

My father said we couldn't afford to have another dog. I said she could eat some of my food. But he was also worried about my mother, still grieving for her dog Sambo, a lively black Cocker Spaniel that was killed on the railroad tracks while we were gathering coal that fell from the passing railroad cars. Enough pieces would fall to fill our pockets for the coal stove. Sambo never listened and ran in front of the train. My mother was devastated by the loss and my father didn't think she would want another dog. But Bambi was so meek and loving that he relented. After a small flutter of protests and the fact that Mittens took a liking to her, she was given entrance to our family.

I had never wanted to leave the city. Germantown was just a short trolley ride to Philadelphia, where there were lots of big libraries with an infinite amount of books. But nonetheless, we moved to a little starter house in Woodbury

Gardens, with a pig farm and swamp to the right, and an unkempt field with an old barn across the road. It was a comfort having my dog in this unknown territory.

We spent long hours together as I explored the small forest lining the edge of our neighborhood. I named all I saw. Red Clay Mountain. Rainbow Creek. Punk Swamp. There was life everywhere, mysterious and energetic. In time I came to cherish our surroundings. We led our Peter Pan existence— Bambi my spirit dog with the deep sad eyes.

Kimberly was often ill. The doctor ordered the house to be stripped of every allergen, including our precious animals. This was a terrible blow, yet I was not without understanding. I had no resentment against the baby or the doctor. We all knew it was our duty to help Kimberly, but the thought of giving up Mittens and Bambi was heartbreaking. I thought of running away with her. But where would we go? I could sleep in the fields shrouded at night with the invisible cloth of the woolgatherers. I could hide in the forest and build a hut in the trees and live like one of the Lost Boys. But I knew I could never run away and leave my siblings. I could never leave Kimberly. Who would rock her when my parents were working? Who would watch her sleep making certain she did not hold her breath and leave us forever?

The day was fast coming when the family offering to take Bambi would arrive. I vaguely knew one of them from school. The idea sickened me. In my heart I felt a possessiveness I had never experienced. I couldn't bear the thought of someone else having my dog.

I got up quite early and left the house with her. It was in my mind to take her to all the places we loved. We would take one last walk to Red Clay Mountain and stop awhile by Rainbow Creek. I had a peanut butter sandwich wrapped in wax paper and some dog biscuits. I sat with Bambi at my feet and surveyed my domain. She would not eat her treats. She knows, I thought. She knows. I stopped trying to hide what was going to happen and I told her everything, without words. I told her through my eyes from my heart. She licked my face and I knew she understood.

Bambi rarely barked. There was only the silence of her sad deer eyes. Soon it was time to go back home. But first I took her to Thomas's Field and we lay in the grass and looked up at the clouds. The sun was warm on my face and I dozed. Bambi slept with her head and paw resting on my chest.

I awoke and knew we had to hurry home. I could feel my mother searching me out. I ran across the field towards home, just across the road. Bambi darted ahead of me. I called her. She stopped suddenly in the middle of the road. I called her again but she stayed still, looking right into my eyes. Even from a distance it was as if I could see my own reflection. I froze. I just stood there as a fire truck came racing from nowhere and struck her.

The fireman stopped and got out. My father rushed from the house and scooped her up, laying her near the bushes. The sacred bushes of God. No one said anything. No one asked what happened. The fireman felt terrible for killing her, but I knew it wasn't his fault.

I knelt down and looked at my dog. She was still warm. There was not a mark on her, not even a drop of blood. It was if she was sleeping, but she was dead. My mother was crying. My sister Linda's astonished blue eyes dominated her compassionate face. I got an old woolen blanket and wrapped her in it. My father buried her by the side of the house as we said our prayers.

I did not cry. The complexity of my feeling so profound that it lifted me above the realm of tears. I ruminated on this day for a long time. Did I wish her dead? Or was it her? Surely she knew. Neither of us wanted her to belong to someone else.

It was Indian summer and the trees were already red and gold. As the days passed I disobeyed my mother and bicycled across the forbidden perimeter to Woodbury to find Harry Riehl. I thought he could solve the riddle that weighed on me so heavily. The riddle of Bambi's death. Harry was the one who had identified the spirits of the field, and I believed he knew the answer to everything. But for the first time he was not at his station guarding his widow. He wasn't there the next time either and I never saw him again.

Sometime later I was holding Kimberly in my arms. She'd had an asthma attack while my parents were out. I tended to her as I was taught then was able to rock her to sleep. I heard some shouting from across the road. The sun was going down and I stepped outside. The old black barn was in flames. I heard a terrible screeching. Someone said it was bats burning alive. I stood there cradling the baby. The sky was purple with golden streaks. I could see the planets and the evening star.

Hovering above the field were swarms of gnats and fireflies. Pale lunar moths circled the night lights, with a life of their own. My brother raced across the road; nothing is more exciting for a young boy than a fire. Yet I knew the flames wouldn't spread. The barn would burn and leave its mark but the field was safe, for the woolgatherers would protect it. Just as Harry Riehl had protected his wife and I was protecting Kimberly. The baby awoke and smiled at me. It occurred to me that nothing was more beautiful than a newborn smile.

Kimberly

The wall is high, the black barn
The babe in my arms in her swaddling clothes
And I know soon that the sky will split
And the planets will shift,
Balls of jade will drop and existence will stop
Little sister, the sky is falling, I don't mind
Little sister, the fates are calling on you

Here I stand again in this old electric whirlwind
The sea rushes up my knees like flame
And I feel like just some misplaced Joan of Arc
And the cause is you looking up at me.
Oh baby, I remember when you were born
It was dawn and the storm settled in my belly
And I rolled in the grass and I spit out the gas
And I lit a match and the void went flash
And the sky split and the planets hit
Balls of jade dropped and existence stopped

Little sister, the sky is falling, I don't mind
Little sister, the fates are calling on you

I was young and crazy, so crazy I knew
I could break through with you
So with one hand I rocked you
With one heart I reached for you.
Ah, I knew our youth was for the taking
Fire on a mental plane
So I ran through the fields as the bats
With their baby veined faces
Burst in flames in the violent violet sky
And I fell on my knees and pressed you against me.
Your soul was like a network of spittle
Like glass balls moving in
Like cold streams of logic
And I prayed as the lightning attacked
That something will make it go crack
Something will make it go crack
The palm trees fall into the sea
It doesn't matter much to me
As long as you're safe, Kimberly
And I can gaze deep
Into your starry eyes
Into your starry eyes

Millet

I never met my grandmothers, as both of them died quite young, the year before I was born. Jessie Smith was a lace maker, played the standing harp and died after a long illness on Palm Sunday. Marguerite Williams, my mother's mother, played the mandolin. By all accounts she was a happy little thing, though afflicted by a madness, and she died alone in an asylum.

I only knew my great-grandmother Olive Hart, who shunned me. She was a tall, stoic woman who, with the early death of her mother, tended to her five siblings. At twenty-five she wed, bore and raised four sons, and then, with Marguerite in the asylum, was obliged to raise my mother and her younger brothers.

My mother did all she could to please her grandmother yet could never gain her favor. When we visited she would do all the laundry by hand on a scrub board connected to

a large metal tub. I could not help but admire her cheerfulness as she wrung out the sheets and hung them to dry in the sun. Then she would linger, smoking a cigarette, to assess her handiwork rippling in the wind. Later I would help her by gathering clothespins as she folded and laid the sweet-smelling linens in a laundry basket. But all her loving toil did not elicit a single smile from Olive Hart.

My great-grandmother took a disliking to me, as she had to my mother. Yet I was more like her than not, as I resembled her sons and had something of her features and standoffish manner. She descended from a long line of Norfolk farmers and solitary shepherds. Her blood contained them and so commingled with mine. I was conscious, even as she slighted me, that through her I possessed the soul of the shepherdess. Through her I was drawn to the dreamers' life and I imagined tending a flock, gathering wool in a leather pouch, and contemplating the color of the clouds.

As fate devised, I pursued a path far afield from my ancestors, yet their ways are also mine. And in my travels, when I see a hill dotted with sheep or a staff lying among the chestnut leaves, I am moved by a sense of longing to be again what I was not.

Flying

It was my mother who taught me to pray. I can still see myself kneeling before my little bed made ready for me with such devotion. My mother also made my pajamas, which were somewhat short as my legs were too long. But I was proud of them for she had made them with her own hand.

After my prayers, when all was still, when I could hear the soft breath of my brother and sister fast asleep, I'd mount a chair and push aside the cloth that covered my window. I would continue my commune while on watch for them — the woolgatherers — clawing the lost so it will be found again, even the most anxious light. And on particularly wondrous nights, when prayer itself seemed an adventure, something would unzip and I'd be off to be among them. I did not run, I'd glide — some feet above the grass. This was my secret ability — my crown.

These times were set apart, unique. The people were not so elusive, darting. Instead they stood in facing lines, making ready, dressed in the cap and cloth of their kind; spun of a trembling thread. They seemed, bathed in pale clairvoyance, less like people than rows of quaking aspen with leaves quivering at the slightest breath. They traced, in concert, the mystery of their work, conspiring in their movements to cleanse and to magnify existence in a song of man. It appeared they were not gathering but giving, and for a moment all the world seemed blessed.

The Lord gives us wings
He gives us a stomach
we can fly or vomit
turn ourselves in glory
turn upon the water
draw a cup of bitters
turn ourselves inside out
and a sum of us
will flicker
just a bit of dust, hardly noticed
but it fills the air with a substance.
The immortal dream ...

They spun their song — a cloth of its own, and I, being young, tired of it and wandered on. Gliding above the grass, sometimes leaving the impression of my hands on the fruits of their labor, stacked like bales of cotton wool here and there. Recycled souls, tears, the babbling of children and crazy laughter. All this I would touch or poke with my finger, releasing a fragrant if not hallowed mist.

And what I gathered there I let fly again save for a small part to present as garlands for my brother and sister who often awoke when I returned.

They slept until their sleep turned to water. They awoke and their awaking was the cracking of an egg. All that I had

seen and heard I described to them, and their bold believing hearts spurred me on. Perhaps I held back something of the people, this being, I perceived, one of the silences. But of all my journeys — the bright passages, marble lace, the fabled arch and the great cloak that opened onto Kansas, Siam ...

All this I came to report.

And when we grew and were obliged to part I no longer had them to report my goings to. I wrote, I drew, or let them fly. Oblivious to any design save the simple act of landing in the nettle and being snapped up by a gatherer with compassion for the small.

Time passes and with it certain sensations. Yet once in a while the magic of the field and all that happened there surfaces. Not necessarily in nature but within the leaves of a book, the painting of Millet or the tones of a Corot. Wandering through the long gallery hall, in a light decidedly Dutch, it comes to me. I see myself alight upon the meadow, and feel as I felt — clear, unspeakable joy.

A snake in the grass with wings ...

I had taken this gift for granted as children do. I forgot about it, never tested it. It was just one of those rare, simple things I knew to be true.

Not long ago I had a dream. If one must call certain experiences dream. In Thomas' Field on a clear autumn afternoon. On this patch of land, seemingly abandoned, while my brother and sister sat watching in wordless admiration, I leapt suspended a few feet above the ground. I did not fly but hovered, like a saucer, like Nijinsky, and somehow it seemed in its simplicity all the more miraculous. Still not a word was spoken, as was common between us. A communion bred of love and innocence.

I awoke with well-being and was happy all day until bending to a chore it occurred to me that I had merely dreamed. Caught in this fading strain I tumbled. Yet I felt that once I had been truly capable of this modest incredible feat and could be again if I willed so.

Having had a glass of tea, filled with optimism, I could almost be persuaded to try it just once. My moccasins seem fit for the task. And the urge is there, to test an irresistible skill. But my writing desk awaits, my open journal, my

quills, inks, and there are precious words to grind. So I leave myself to wonder and begin, for I always imagined I would one day write a book.

Above my desk is a small portrait — Flemish, fifteenth-century. It never fails, when I gaze upon it, to produce a shudder, followed by a curious rush of warmth, recognition. Perhaps it is the serenity of expression or perhaps the head-covering — a fragile habit framing the face like the folding wings of a large, diaphanous moth.

A Farewell

The air was carnival, responsive. I opened the screen door and stepped out. I could feel the grass crackle. I could feel life — a burning coal tossed on a valentine of hay. I covered my head. I would gladly have covered my arms, face. I stood and watched the children at play and something in the atmosphere — the filtered light, the scent of things — carried me back...

How happy we are as children. How the light is dimmed by the voice of reason. We wander through life — a setting without a stone. Until one day we take a turn and there it lies on the ground before us, a drop of faceted blood, more real than a ghost, glowing. If we stir it may disappear. If we fail to act nothing will be reclaimed. There is a way in this little riddle. To utter one's own prayer. In what manner it doesn't matter. For when it is over that person shall possess the only jewel worth keeping. The only grain worth giving away.

A small hand offered me a dandelion.

Make a wish!

I took it. A yellow bright — wild, insignificant and beloved by God. Transforming for the sake of our desire into an ancient puff. Bits of fuzzy manna descend upon the world ...

Make a wish, blow ...

Having my breath what more could I wish for. All of my being rose in this pursuit. I had the advantage of the sky with its ability to become, in the twinkling of an eye, everything.

I searched the clouds for omens, answers. They seemed to be moving very fast, dome-shaped, delicate, connective tissue. The face of art, in profile. The face of denial, blessed.

What do we do Great Barrymore?
We stagger
What shall we do simple monk?
Be of good heart

And these words of advice, imparted with such undivided grace, filled my limbs with such a lightness that I was lifted and left to glide above the grass, although it appeared to all that I was still among them, wrapped in human tasks, with both feet on the ground.

Afterthoughts

Make a wish!

My little daughter approached me with the fuzzy head of a dandelion—*Blow!*

Much time has passed since that summer afternoon in Michigan. Now my daughter is grown, yet my wishes for her, as she navigates the edges of our troubled world, have not changed.

When conceiving *Woolgathering*, I wrote in the kitchen at a small card table by the screen door. I could hear the laughter of the children playing. It was in the early nineties and my husband was quite ill. We traveled very little, yet as I wrote, in the solitude of my kitchen, I was able to roam freely the scarcely charted landscape of memory governed by clouds.

Now, in the time of the pandemic, the parameters of our travels are set by the virus. The physical laws of our movements are no longer governed by choice, but placed upon us. During quarantine, lockdown and our restricted present, I often combat restlessness by plowing through boxes of Polaroid images and nostalgically revisiting the provinces of former journeys, when my work took me from city to city across a global map.

Casting a mental dart toward that map I find myself randomly landing in the Basque country, on the southern coast of the Bay of Biscay. I was there with my comrades a year ago, ending a concert tour of Portugal and Spain. We were heading toward the French border but stopped overnight in San Sebastián. There was the promise of the sea, but I also wished to see the statue of the city's namesake, a statue standing in a niche beneath the great clock on the exterior of the Basilica of Saint Mary. Night was approaching, but the statue, pierced with arrows, could be seen illuminated by golden floodlights. We were surprised to find that a crowd had gathered, all looking toward the sky expectantly, as if awaiting a celestial phenomenon. Discovering we had unknowingly arrived during the great annual firework competition, we sat on the stone steps to watch the spectacle with the others.

Toward the finale, the full moon suddenly burned through clouds of smoke. All gasped at its majestic appearance, a full super moon, eclipsing the successive bursts of artificial shooting stars. Walking back to the hotel, the moon hovering above us, I lagged behind, silently conversing with it as I have done so often since a child.

I awoke early, downed my coffee and hurriedly revisited the Basilica alone. Etched in morning light the statue of Saint Sebastián seemed to mirror Michelangelo's *Dying Slave*, both muscular young men with an arm raised above their heads—one stilled by arrows, one in chains—projecting beauty and vitality in the face of death.

I rejoined my comrades, we had our last repast in Spain then crossed the border and drove to the coastal town of Biarritz. Having no further work obligations, I bid my friends farewell and stayed alone for a few days in a small hotel adjacent to the Crypt of Saint Eugenie. I had no plans save to manage a pleasant routine and hopefully write. At twilight I sat on my small balcony and read, pausing for several moments to admire the view of the lighthouse. I could feel an approaching storm and through the night I listened to the distant thunder; the flashing signal of the lighthouse merged with lightning and could be seen through the glass doors.

I awoke early, had breakfast on the patio and sat musing on how to spend my day. A small group of pilgrims gathered by the Crypt and young people were wholeheartedly recruiting tourists to join a procession celebrating the feast day of the Assumption of Mary. I was recruited twice. First by a somewhat ragged but affable boy with unruly hair and enormous dark eyes, flanked by his dog. The boy declared themselves homeless, bringing to mind the orphaned lad Nello and his dog Patrasche, in Ouida's *Dog of Flanders*. It had once been a favorite book of mine, a woeful tale of a poor Flemish orphan, starving and cold, seeking refuge with his faithful dog in the Cathedral of Our Lady. On Christmas night, in the swirl of snow and celebration, both succumb at the foot of a majestic Rubens.

Patient with my momentary reverie, he handed me a flyer announcing that the processional would proceed at 9 p.m. from the crypt of St. Eugenie to the Roche de la Vierge.

"Have you said hello to the bear of Biarritz?" he asked.

"No, should I?"

"Oh yes, he is not far and smiles on tourists."

I followed him around a wide curve, up a hill past a bakery to find a life-size, welcoming bear on vigil from a second-floor balcony. I waved, thanking the bear for watching over the likes of me, said farewell and gave the boy a few euros and watched him go on his way with his dog, whistling.

Soon after a young girl offered me a length of white yarn adorned with a silver-colored medal of Our Lady, explaining in broken English that I should wear it during the candlelight procession. I slipped it around my neck, an unconfirmed vow—I knew I could not join them. She walked away then turned and sunnily smiled. I felt as if we had met before, a trick of flickering memory, the moment superimposing itself over a similar one in a film. A lingering shot of a wistful girl with a flaxen ponytail calling to Marcello on the beach toward the end of *La Dolce Vita*. Drawn away by his companions, he stumbles on ahead, then turns; she smiles, with all the dazzling openness of youth.

Having accepted the necklace, I decided to take the processional route on my own while it was yet light. I had to go at my own pace, due to my excessive clumsiness when ascending and descending multiple stairs, and there were many. With some hesitancy I proceeded unguided, up and down steps of stone and wood, following winding paths

through wild patches of aloe, yucca, hanging jasmine, twist-ing trees, and clusters of multicolored Hortense. A lengthy though worthy undertaking, if only to experience a myriad of scents, the last breath of fading lavender.

At last the Virgin's Rock rose in the distance, a white statue perched atop an observation deck facing the old harbor. Grateful seafarers had erected the statue in 1865, as an ex-tension of the mystical light said to emanate from the rocky outcrop. Surrounded by water and crashing waves, the sight of it served as a munificent protector, warning sailors and fisherman away from shipwreck.

To reach the rock I was obliged to cross a small iron foot-bridge, designed by Eiffel, replacing a more precarious wooden one built in the time of Napoleon III. Having an irrational fear of footbridges, I sat on a nearby bank gather-ing a bit of courage. The light was changing; soon the for-mal procession for the *Assumption* would begin, a long line of worshipers wearing her likeness on lengths of yarn, hold-ing fast to their candles, winding the same challenging path.

It was a beautiful evening. I sat for a while recalling the sanc-tified models of the death of Mary. The *Assumption* denotes all earthly life is finished; she is assumed body and soul to join her son in heaven. Her ascension was rendered in the early seventeenth century by the artist Rubens for the high altar of the Cathedral of our Lady in Antwerp: the same Cathedral where the freezing boy Nell and his dog, ignored by passersby, sought refuge, with nothing save the splendidly Baroque hand of Rubens to comfort them.

The *Dormition*, celebrated by the Orthodox, attests that she does not die, she sleeps. El Greco composed a vision of the *Dormition* in the Cathedral of the Dormition Hermoupolis in the town of Hermes. Using the falling colors of autumn, in tempera and gold, he depicts the sleep of the queen of heaven, ordained to unite with her son in an age to come.

Somewhat earlier, around 1604, the artist Caravaggio gave us the most moving image of the death of the Virgin. He abandoned the traditional blue robe and golden girdle, the winged seraphim and grieving apostles, drawing instead from the chambers of the human heart. She lays with her right hand resting beneath her breast and the left slightly dangling from the edge of her parapet. Neither assumption nor holy sleep, she is purely dead, adorned in a red cloth reminiscent of John the Baptist's cloak, shrouded in emotional silence.

I finally gathered the courage and crossed the footbridge. I gazed at the solitary statue, a symbol of humility, pleased to have accomplished my mission. Beneath a canopy of bruised yet billowing clouds was the sea, its foam crashing the rocks of volcanic slag. In the distance, an indistinct view of the sloping Basque mountains.

All about was the hum of believers, the whispers of lovers and the giddy laughter of children. I sat on a nearby bench and quietly prayed, asking that her maternal love be magnified on their behalf. That was over a year ago and my prayers have not altered. We pray for our young, pulled from promising paths in the wake of the pandemic, indigenous children of the Amazon where rainforests burn, children in Yemen trapped in an epidemic of mass starvation, and in East Africa where a plague of locusts of Biblical proportion devours all crops and sustainable hopes.

All children are our children. These words floated in a mild breeze. I stood for a few moments, watching the little ones at play, racing up and rolling down the green hill where a cross is mounted, slightly obscured by the pines.

The procession advanced. Searching a mental catalogue of beloved music, I caught some of the melodious strains of Massenet's oratorio *Le Dernier Sommeil*—the last sleep. The air was like milk; harmonies breathed in concert with the sea. I was suddenly quite tired and unconsciously tugged at the little medal hanging from the length of yarn as if it had the power to beam me back onto the little balcony of my hotel.

How shall I yield? That was my thought as I sat on the bench, closing my eyes for just a moment, then opening them in time to catch a glimpse of the homeless boy and his dog crossing the footbridge. He noticed me, waved then continued on toward the Virgin, now crowned by cumulus clouds. All at once, the mornings lying in the high grass of Thomas's field, with my dog at my side, came flowing back. So many hours spent gazing at such clouds and imagining the comings and goings of its sacred inhabitants. Those memories begat others as I followed my mental arrow back in time to the realm of the Woolgatherers. I could see them, as night fell, in their Flemish hats, opening their aprons to collect bits of trembling spirits that had gone astray, flittering about them like bewildered moths.

NEW YORK CITY, DECEMBER 2020

Illustrations

77. *Jesse Smith, African daisy, 2004*, Patti Smith, 2004.

82. *St. Sebastián*, Patti Smith, 2019.

84. *The Bear of Biarritz*, Patti Smith, 2019.

86. *The Virgin's Rock, Biarritz*, Patti Smith, 2019.

89. *Death of the Virgin* (detail), Caravaggio.

92. *The author in Thomas's Field*, Linda Smith Bianucci, c. 1996.

All photos courtesy of the author.